Albert E. Scheflen, M.D.

is Professor of Psychiatry
at Albert Einstein College of Medicine
and Researcher in Human Communication
at the Bronx State Hospital
and Jewish Family Service.

Alice Scheflen

has been a feature writer and editor
in medicine and the sciences
and Research
Assistant in
Human Communication.